LIFE UNDER WATER

Maura Dooley was born in Truro, grew up in Bristol, and after working for some years in Yorkshire moved to London. She is a freelance writer and lectures at Goldsmiths' College. She edited *Making for Planet Alice: New Women Poets* (1997) and *The Honey Gatherers: A Book of Love Poems* (2002) for Bloodaxe, and *How Novelists Work* (2000) for Seren. *Life Under Water* (Bloodaxe Books, 2008) is a Poetry Book Society Recommendation and her first new collection since *Sound Barrier: Poems 1982-2002* (Bloodaxe Books, 2002), which drew on collections including *Explaining Magnetism* (1991) and *Kissing a Bone* (1996), both also Poetry Book Society Recommendations. *Kissing a Bone* was shortlisted for the T.S. Eliot Prize.

MAURA DOOLEY

Life
Under
Water

BLOODAXE BOOKS

Copyright © Maura Dooley 2008

ISBN: 978 1 85224 817 8

First published 2008 by
Bloodaxe Books Ltd,
Highgreen,
Tarset,
Northumberland NE48 1RP.

www.bloodaxebooks.com
For further information about Bloodaxe titles
please visit our website or write to
the above address for a catalogue.

Bloodaxe Books Ltd acknowledges
the financial assistance of
Arts Council England, North East.

Cover design: Neil Astley & Pamela Robertson-Pearce.

Printed in Great Britain by
Bell & Bain Limited, Glasgow, Scotland.

A.M.
1954–2008

ACKNOWLEDGEMENTS

Acknowledgements are due to the editors of the following publications in which some of these poems, or versions of them, first appeared: *After Thirty Falls: New Essays on John Berryman*, edited by Philip Coleman & Philip McGowan (Rodopi, 2007), *In Person: 30 Poets*, filmed by Pamela Robertson-Pearce & edited by Neil Astley (Bloodaxe Books, 2008), *New Welsh Review*, *The North*, *Out of Fashion*, edited by Carol Ann Duffy (Faber & Faber, 2004), *Poetry*, *Poetry Ireland*, *Poetry Jukebox*, *Poetry Review*, *Signs and Humours: The Poetry of Medicine*, edited by Lavinia Greenlaw (Calouste Gulbenkian Foundation, 2007), *Smiths Knoll* and *The Times Educational Supplement*.

A version of 'The Source' was commissioned by Tim Dee for BBC Radio 4. 'Mummy' was commissioned by Julian May for BBC Radio 3. 'The 1984 Perspective' was commissioned by the National Railway Museum and Paul Munden for the NAWE *Moving Stories* project. 'The Lark Ascending' was commissioned by Tom Hutchinson for the Royal Philharmonic Society for their *Hear Here!* project.

Thank you to several dear friends and to my family. I am indebted to Jonathan Davidson. Thank you always, David Hunter.

CONTENTS

Dear, I know nothing of
Either, but when I try to imagine a faultless love
Or the life to come, what I hear is the murmur
Of underground streams, what I see is a limestone landscape.

W.H. AUDEN, 'In Praise of Limestone'

The World Turned Upside Down

To break and lift a frozen pane

and see my city made strange,
now, in these warming streets,
the way fires at Frost Fair once
made all that was constant tremble,
a shiver of flame, fire on ice, 1643,
the country shook as it watched.

Just as the glint of refraction
distorts the story handed down
of how a skein of snow locked
a ship into ice at Nova Zembla,
bitter weeks of past and future
held in the long cold of the moment.

How did they dream in that white
echo? Everything drained, thinned
to a blankness, pattern that lost
all pattern, a bleakness that took
Wilson Bentley a lifetime to define.
Snowflake, no two ice flowers alike.

Oh, my poor language,
that offers so many words for snow
but never the weather to use them,
only this damp longing for silence
that is sleet, that is slush, that might be
a city made strange, life under water.

Dulwich Picture Gallery through a Veil of Tears

Not a valley exactly, more the morose plains of south London,
the snow masked our way and the tears that coursed your face
    constant,
unstemmed, unremarked through your ache of missing her missing
    her
made everything muted, padded, watery-white, made this life as
    nothing,

which left us art. The lights were necessarily dim, the glass present
    if non-reflective,
so we were unable to see how it was done exactly, were there pencil
    marks?
Your swimming vision may have added something to the conviction,
and I, too brimful of you and your lack of her, felt grateful just to
    believe in it.

When we stepped from the carefully measured warmth back into
    January air
to find our tracks covered completely, nothing behind us, the road
    ahead a blank,
the engine cold, we shivered together. Then pulling onto the road
    in those moments
before headlights are needed, I lit a cigarette for you, something else
    you'd given up.

The Elevator

As an oyster opens,
wondrous, and through mud
lets glitter that translucent
promise, so the lift doors
close and I am inside
alone with Leonard Cohen.

Vertigo, fear, desire.
I could unpeel myself here,
not just down to honest
freckled skin but through
the sticky layers of a past.

Surely he'd know me anywhere?

Remember that time in the Colston Hall,
how you sang only to me?

The Albert Hall, when I blagged
a press seat and you never once
took your eyes from my shining face?

Here, now, today, in Toronto,
how did you find me?
How did you know I'd be here?

He looks to where I stand
in the radiant silence,
the earth falling away beneath us,
till the silvery gates slide open
to release him. He steps out.
He steps out and I stand still.

'D'you know where you're going?'
he asks.
'Is this where you wanted to be?'

From Where I Stand

The comma
        and the full stop
                afloat
on my childish horizon
            are islands,
Flat and Steep,
       and if, on a clear day,

I walk the pier at Clevedon,
             mended now,
sound,
    someone might ask
           and I'd say *no*,
I have never,
      would like to,
           have wanted to,
used to imagine even
          the way birds would cry
and clatter,
      not sing as they did back home,

safe amidst the apples of the Beauty of Bath,
                      no,
loud and keening,
       then, after the rough crossing,

how I would scramble
          with grassy knees,

effortful   breathless,

only to turn at the top, turn and look back

at the coast,
      diminished,
         oh, just a speck in the eye.

Last night: showers, fierce winds.
Hung over, despite sleep,
I quiz the young maid.
'The quince is fine' she shrugs,
O, can't you see?
Green leaves shoot, blossom falls.

LI QINGZHAO (Sung Dynasty)

four chambers

Valentine

His, over the mantelpiece,
heaved out for all to see,
I grew up with.

Yours, I had only felt
in thought and deed,
an insistent patterning
when we lie like spoons at night,

Corazón, coeur,
kindness, the core of you.

Year Eight Science

The Halal butcher took care,
wrapping it several times,
still, there was bound to be
blood,
      in the dish, on her gloves.

The chambers of this new house
were unclear,
      the walls unsteady
as she was now, cloudy-headed,
willing the knife to be sure.

What She Called the Blood Jet

The cabinet of love has only two doors,
in and out. There are four rooms.
In the first, screwtop bottles and foil strips
hold brilliantly coloured answers.
The second holds something French
to do with herbs and truffle.
The third has the memory of childhood
and here, last of all, like mica, like mercury,
lies the present. It is a muscle. It is meat.

Stent!

Dearest Heart,
'felt, 'rending, 'broken,
it's what I know you by.

                              Repeat
again and again
                    please repeat.

Angina Pectoris rustles her wings
and all the old familiar words
are under attack.

                    Let's edit.
Let's make one tiny, precise
amendment and leave the work
as it always was, perfect.

                         *   *   *

UnIrished

Your name is important. It's like your face or your smile or your skin.
HUGO HAMILTON

Oh my name it is nothin', my age it means less.
BOB DYLAN

      Place of birth?
You raise it
like a hedge of
             furze
between us.
         See,
I even have to pause
to find the word
you grew with.

Know me then
by the burden
of my hair,
my marbled skin
that
         burns,

my memory.

What You Will

It was cold and a sound kept me awake
startled and startling. It was cold,
Christmas came and went with
its child and donkey, sheep and lonely star.
And still, nightly, an unbuttoned cry
rasped on the frosty street.
                              Lifting the curtain
on darkness, mist rising from the Common,
I saw nothing, nothing, and lay awake till morning.

So, it was you, Twelfth Night, 4.00 A.M.,
home from the hospital, where we, still swaddled, slept,
it was you, who braked slowly, just outside,
coming to stop before the golden gaze of fox.

Fox.
    Fox in a halo of light, fox who chose
that icy morning to reveal herself
to stop you in your tracks, to open her soft throat
and let out that strange, familiar cry.
It was cold
              and her voice slewed the trees silver,
glazed the shivering grasses, rose glittering up, up,
through particles of stars to where the Magi,
heavy with their gifts, finally laid them down in golden light.

Midsummer Lullaby

Nights like these,
the almost days when sleep won't come
or drifts in, fitful, with you, castaway,
beached on steep heat, tall light,
even in this pale summer darkness
wanting still the comfort of a lamp.

Here, where electricity never fails,
stars are bleached out,
matches wait for bonfire night,
candles for birthdays,
a ceramic moon hangs by your bed.

Nights like these,
the almost days when sleep won't come
and you, calling out, reaching out,
for a lamp to scratch the dark,
are small enough still, to make do instead
with any little light my hand might shed.

Lettered

I'm looking back to where my father stands
at the souvenir shop by the bend of a lane,
kitchenware printed with lines from *Jane Eyre*
or a verse in dialect strung on the wind. 'Come on!'
He is deep in a teatowel and has to finish.

'Shoes! Hair! Teeth! It's a quarter to nine!'
Another sweet mild head that does not stir,
she's only just starting her story
and another page is turned.
Is this how Alexandria burned?

Her younger sister sharpens a crayon,
prints seagulls onto blue sky,
so many of them, gathering low
over her pencilled house, the body of each bird
a true spine, wings bent open, ready, taking off.

Moth Trap

We looked to learn,
lit the lamp, waited
till something like a bloom
could be gathered,
its freedom tethered
by a shaft of light,

the way this lovely girl,
observing her own shadow,
holds up twelve years of life,
complicated filigree,
a thread leading home,
a rope to be cast off.

Self-portrait in a Velvet Dress

(Frida Kahlo, 1926)

Instead, let me tell you of *my* earlier version,
aged nine or ten, how I loved it!
Chocolate brown, satin trim, gathered to the waist,
family party, a perfect fit.

Cut up for dusters, I still have one or two
and pause at ten to nine,
shocked, as I buff to a shine a daughter's shoe,
by the face that looks back clear from it

at me, on my knees, as at a shrine,
the hair unschooled, the way the dark brows knit.

a work in four movements (unfinished)

Prelude

A white butterfly visits the rosemary bush.
Its hesitation on the tricky leaves
throws up a fragrance seen through glass.

Opening the door on the scent of remembrance,
September sunshine, promise, he knows
the moment before it all looked just like this.

The Old Masters

You'll know the photograph,
legs dangling from girders,
spik, polak, yid, paddy, nigger, wop,
the Rockefeller Building, rising like sap,
how, freed from one hell or another,
                              tempest-tost,
they washed up at *the golden door*.

There is more than one tower
in which language might ferment.

We never knew how many
till we saw it in the papers,
names from every land
thrown across the news
of every land.
                    The many tongues
in the one tower, in the more
than one tower, hanging,
                    as they do,
hanging in Rotterdam and Vienna,
in student flats, church halls, cafés,
in another painting by Brueghel.

There are towers that make gods jealous
towers that make men jealous
and there are tongues,
                    those that ask,
those silenced, those not yet understood,
                              those lost,
those I have to strain to hear,

not wanting ever again to see
Something amazing, a boy falling out of the sky.

The Final Stages of Diplomacy

(Dick Cheney, March 2003)

On the asphalt they argue about positions,
one puts down a bag to mark the spot,
the next wants to know what is in the bag.
Someone else comes now, stands silently,
saying nothing, his hands loose at his sides,
he says nothing, and then they start to push.

We make our little murmuring noises
of restraint, we smile or look anxious.
It goes on and it is the bag's fault,
this pushing. If only someone
would open the bag (Look! Empty!)
or take it away, it doesn't need to be there.

If only the bell would go.

If only Sir would come,
(nonchalant, only slightly late)
to usher them inside, orderly,
the bags all checked and safely stowed,
then Circle Time on the carpet,
Show and Tell, prayers.

After Diplomacy

He does not speak
and when he moves his head
I see it clear,
            his face as mapwork,
ridges and furrows,
                    glasswork,
an A-Z of misfortune.

He turns away again,
the other cheek,
a clean uncomplicated surface
and does not speak.

*   *   *

Strange Meeting

(in memory of Michael Donaghy)

The late train back,
                      me quiet with a book,
the Stopping train's stopping,
                 I stop to look.

A quarter mile of skid and hiss then this –

your face out of the black night air,
our faces, all reflection, meeting in the glass,
a moment of connection, then it's past.

Retford maybe, Seamer, Crewe,
I don't remember, just it was you.

You got on my train.

Last train into St Pancras
                      and no one there,
no one there but us laughing
and sparkling
                 in the lamplight's steady glare
dust.
     If there's somewhere
out beyond the bended knee
that you and I were forged with
I hope to see you. I hope to see

your face against the black night air,
the ice, the rain, your face again.

Get on my train.

Leaf

(in memory of John McGahern)

Leaf light on the morning lane
was the heart's needle,

spangle of cloud and water
glitter enough.

A word spoken, a word withheld,
tells your story,

splinter of ice, splinter of grief,
splinter of love.

In which Paula loses an earring and has it restored to her

(for PM & TD)

An orb spinning
                    slips from its ken,
from your certain touch,
                    and is lost.
We search all that can be held
try to picture all that cannot.

It matters terribly at such a moment,
this shift in your earth's axis,
the disappearance of a nameless planet.

Good then, that at the water's edge
                                    and just in time,
ornament resurfaces as lucky charm.

You hold it now, in trembling hands, joyous.

Love does this to us,
shows us its darker side as loss.

For now, your head is straight again,
you are well-balanced.
Those earrings catch the happy salty light.

Culver Hole Smuggler

SS46538457

Here is a cave,
         a slither of karst,
a cove and
         spirits in a bottle
bright stories claim
         for this sliver of dark.

I prefer
the song of an anchorite,
rising
         like the lark

in lambent air,

a brace to all
that is soft or shallow,

         glistening, sharp,

her days rinsed clear
at All Hallows
         by stormlight,
moonbeam,
         salt's secret mark.

Jansson's Temptation

Remember the Englishman
who showed us round that glittering city,
listing not the more than twenty different kinds of herring
but the seven unsolved murders?

It set our teeth on edge.

Remember the glogg that warmed our hands
amongst the guttering flames of the old square?

Snow steady over Skansen,

Storkyrkan brilliant with song,
the townhall afloat in moonlight,

a bayful of islands glimmering, glass, water?

Or maybe you remember what we ate that night,
how potato and fish came together, melting finally
the vowels and consonants that had kept our tongues apart.

Smash the Windows

or, Ten South London Fiddle Tunes

1. The Misted Pane
2. Egg on a Bap
3. Knock at the Door
4. A Draught of Air
5. Turd on the Step
6. Fox in a Wheelie Bin
7. Toke on the Swings
8. Parakeet in the Oak
9. The Short Way Home.
10. Glass on the Pavement.

Familiar Object Seen from an Unusual Angle

Maybe it's the surface of the moon, pocky as rind, foreign,
or rain, on the beaches of childhood,
making holes in the sand, the 007 kind, splashy,

or the cross-hatched stars on your hand growing older,
or the real things, sparking still, as they cool,
it's how they twinkle, how we wonder what they are.

Mummy

In his dream, anxiety sends him
to ask just how I plan to solve
the problem at the British Museum.
He finds me ironing but cannot remember what.
I can guess. We'd be in the Egyptian Room,
the bandages spilling out across the floor,
their creases tighter and each coil
steadily more soiled. There is a mist
of steam and hot silver,
light that unspools its greenish net
and there, my arm's compulsive certain strike,
back forth back forth back.
In my homespun way
I am unravelling something foreign to me.
Smoothing out the layers
down to the heart of it, a kernel of jewels,
curses, secrets, love, death, theft.

La Rebeca

Last night I dreamt of the girl who gave her name
to a Spanish cardigan, giving not her own name
but that of a ghost. She is looking back,
back, beyond Manderley, to the idea of a past.

She's no one you could name, this slight and dowdy girl,
the girl who would one day give another's name to a cardigan,
a girl so certain sure in the end of love, of mutability,
of the swan within, that all the ladies of Spain as one
threw off their shawls and wrapped their lovely breasts,
in lambswool, cashmere, a row of seed pearl buttons.
That girl looks back, past Manderley, to the idea of a future,
railings, the war, then another war and the next,
to this woman, now, breath held at the sight of a coal black,
crepe suit, French seamed, an exquisite cut. *Try it*,
the shop voice says, and she does. *It isn't really me.*

So in her shadowy closet, like a fire banked for the night,
it waits, for the moment when that woman decides
for a second time, not to be herself. She will dream.
Then the fire will spark up, the ashes blow toward us,
blow toward us, with the salt wind from the sea.

Suburban Grammar 1968

No toys but a dog in the house with laurels.

Her immaculate face, her heels
a careful click on the icy path,
her car, its door,
the exhalation of leather,
was the proper punctuation of the morning.

His constitutional, the black poodle
in a blue jacket, *The Evening Post*'s
three neat stars, the jagged spear of Venus
above him, that sudden shower of sodium,
the perfect syntax of lighting-up time.

Day-in, day-out, the creak of ice in gin,
work, the unfinished sentence that hung between.

Urban Grammar 2008

He writes of a new girlfriend, Nance,
who used to tuck up with a *Times*
correspondent but now has seen through
the mirrors on that ceiling, decided
instead to slum it here with him.

She has a red sports car (he underlines <u>red</u>),
cool suits and just remembers <u>cool</u>
from the last time around. Therefore,
she is older, wiser, and, his dear friend
Sarah says, looks as if she can handle him.

But Margot, whom he says he loves,
still keeps him at arm's length,
and *My arms will not stretch to Manchester*,
he sighs, *though I keep offering to try*.

There is a pause in his letter here,
deeper than the new paragraph.

Sometimes she seems only to exist,
he writes, in my letters to you.

The Lark Ascending

Nigel Kennedy is in the kitchen,
where all best talk happens,
trying to tell me something,

I think he wants to bring me
late spring at Llanmadoc,
on my back, in clover, reading

invisible ink on a blue page,
at my ear the tick, tick
of an ant's path through grass,

no, he wants to tell me of the murder
of larks, not an exaltation,
three thousand slaughtered daily,

mostly sent to France,
no, no, elongated arpeggio,
listen can't you!

something wants to be said
then said and said again,
something I can't catch,

can't see at all,
till the song comes clear,
till the whole thing flickers,

tumbles, spirals, stroboscopic,
drops like a stone,
falls as news, the edge of everything,

that rap on the door,
the shout from upstairs,
my thoughts that will not settle

long enough to let the full strings
back him up. The milkman on the step
has Neil Young on his radio

and something in that soaring
Heart of Gold lets Nigel Kennedy
smile at me

over the hum of milkfloat,
the whirr and weight of memory,
his tricky, shimmering flight towards the new.

At Liberty

Thief of the morning's shine,
dew-sipper, whose beady eye
is one more bright disc in
a mirrorwork of jet, amethyst,
iridescent silken sequin,
hush that snippy, starveling beak!

Dance in your suit of lights!

The season's short, the trees begin to bare,
in bars of sun and shade the end is near.

Starling Roost

(for Jamie McKendrick)

Here are the sky nails
they asked you for
so long ago

and this their purpose,

in fixing our eyes
to the heavens a moment
the heart lifts.

The Director's Cut

'Never were seen such ruffles, or such embroidered lappets!
But his button-holes were the greatest triumph of it all.'
BEATRIX POTTER,
The Tailor of Gloucester

Your art is the scent of woodsmoke at bitter dusk,
or the mouth's tart cherry in too early a summer,
it is want, blood staining the earth

or rain, rain, rain.
Your eye is the needle through which we all must slip,
your stitches invisible. We are in the doll's house
and you move us.

I am here.

I am there.

My heart is my mouth is my throat is on fire.
My eyes are banked with tears, no, blank with boredom
and we do this again and again. We do this for you.
Then watch you make the untrue true

the true more true.

By Air

If I want to blush
I think of your wallet,
not a lock of hair
but words, my old words,
whatever they were,
folded into four and kept
till they crack along the creases
or the ink rubs away
and each character is released,
a flock of birds wheeling,
that distant calling,
the failure to alight.

Letter in Green Ink

The words insinuate themselves.
Even as you push them away,
shake them off, laugh,
even as you toss them on the fire,
press delete, delete, they are slipping
past the borders of good sense
into unmarked territory,
safely held, for that lonely time,
when they swim to the surface,
solid, unforgettable, right there.

Remark

We had been a long time busy
a little sad maybe,
                                    preoccupied,
then I said something *dry*
perhaps you'd call it

and you laughed
                            in a way
that made me
                        stop and stare.

Sudden, rich and startling
                            it turned my head
and such a flood of happiness was there

that here was something I could do.
Something I'd forgotten I could do.

Here, take it from me,
                                    breathe on it
till it shines
                        and on a darker day
we might see the world more kindly
through it   it might light the way.

Transit

(for John Berryman)

Untidy life of faith and fear and the unfaith
stretch your sexy span across the city
an unforgiving breath from birth to bitter
for he'll remember every slight and kindness
and know that we will likely someday mutter

– I never heard why
Or just how, it was something to do with a bridge –

underwhich flows it all ever endlessly
water traffic the dreams the deep the certainty that
untidy love has him as its sweet kernel
faithless fearless frightened closing the circle
singing *Tomorrow we'll do our best, our best*
Tomorrow we'll do our best.

A Tune for Dave Smith

Call it an interlude, this quiet
that passed between us. Not silence,
the thinking heart can never manage that,
maybe it's what's meant by *intermezzo*.
Well, what can I give you now
that you haven't heard already?
Our household chat, piano practice,
the cackle of crows on the Common,
a train's soft slip into sidings opposite,
the lament of a hungry fox at 2.00 A.M.?
The tune you want to hear is who we are.
If only I could send you that
the water might be still for a moment,
I would walk over it to see you.

The 1984 Perspective

the enemy within (Margaret Thatcher, Orgreave)

Spoil. Slag, packed like sand dunes
all the way down the line to the coast
where coal, washed up on the beach,
handsome and useful, is scavenged
for a little warmth in a long winter.

Meltdown. Rolling stock, gone to Japan
for cars. Meltdown. The blur when
you can't tell who is moving: them or us.

Think of it now and what you see is not
the whole story but the seam of something
precious gone underground, a darkly silver trail
glistening as it vanishes. That's the point.

May 1997

Not her sleepy, puzzled face
accepting flowers
in a dazzle of cameralight,

not his beaming, bemused
thanks
nor the all-day-ticker-tape speeches,

but the easing out of their portable
clothes rail,
shirts and dresses (just like ours!)

swinging, nuzzling and that cheerful,
hopeful,
tinkling sound, that hangers make.

May 2007

London clay gone hard.
All the foolishness of it!
Dust beneath our feet.

Crepuscule

Heavy weather gathers
railway dust, different dirts,
to a trickle
        that finds
              the inside of a collar,

or floods this field
to the shape of a nation
waiting for winter sun
to gain height
        and lift away the worst of it.

Some kind of present
might be revealed in
        a sheep's horn,
a bucket of rust,

or here, where a farmer ploughed
a deft ellipse,
        to leave in summer
a tree afloat on an island of barley,
sun and rain
        manufacturing
viridian and russet. Now,

naked, a shape so particular
           stands clear,
it might be saying

Here I am! The last elm in England!

I will run across these raw furrows
deck the boughs with tincan hopes,
frail prayers,
        as December sun goes down
on a field of winter wheat.

The Source

It is the breaking of the waters that begins it all.

On the Somerset Levels in early Spring,
you might just imagine that basket of canes,
the one perhaps you learned of in school,
an intricacy of withies and moss.
Sphagnum and cottongrass under the head
of the baby entrusted to blue sky and grace,
whose crib tucked inbetween bulrush and bible,
catches on bramble and borders of sedge
and could be any family secret
cast out to float on bright green duckweed
taking its chance under willow and sunshine.

For one is one and all alone
and evermore shall be so.

In rushlit cottages, they plaited soft mats
for the woman in spate brought to the reeds
unstoppable as a late spring-tide.
Loosestrife as blanket, bunting as lullaby.

And God said, let the waters under the heaven
be gathered together in one place,
and let the dry land appear: and it was so.

It is the breaking of the waters that begins it all.

And here the waters were broken
by something like land: the peaty,
Dutch-worked meadows,
whose soft earth could be mist,
a cow's breath on a frost-licked morning.
Meadows that rise in dawnlight
in an orderly gradation of vapours,
luminous, shining-strange, pearly.
Rhines striping the released fields,
a slither of eels in their amber shallows,
like tiny guy ropes tethering

this waterworld that would be one,
with the shoals of a Somerset sky.

And God made the firmament, and divided the waters
which were under the firmament
from the waters which were above the firmament.

          *

What does it mean when a well runs dry?

We've taken too much,
pumped up, poured out
more than we need and now
in Venice, Bangkok, London,
we are the slippery, subsiding places
of the earth and must learn to manage
what has been given.

This plundering mazy search for water,
this greedy, chaotic irrigation
drove springs back under,
down deep into chalk,
but it is the breaking of the waters that begins it all.

The soil, gravel, sand,
the marl, loam and clay over which
the hand with the hazelwand pauses,
hoping to find that path of connection
the way a trickle finds old rock,
clears an avenue through limestone,
forces every fracture and fissure,
makes any void a conduit for water,
spinning to the speleologists' joy,
a cobweb of caves and at its centre,
the suddenness of a buried river.

Dissolving, as it does in water,
is it limestone that yields
the one landscape that we, the inconstant ones,
are consistently homesick for?

Or is it what the Welsh know best?
This, something more than sickness,
which I catch from time to time
in the way sea glimmers
through trees on a coastal road,
or a dewpond rises quietly
on the Common after rain,
or the river, a sudden stripe of light
is glimpsed down an alleyway,
as if the heart in a flash recalls
the way we used to behave.
a mood we forgot we knew,
the liquid landscapes of hope.

*

What does it mean when a well runs dry?

Sometimes gazing too far
downwards, backwards, inwards,
past the glass that Alice climbed through,
past the gaze of Narcissus,
struggling to see a human face,
one reflection or another,
something in the dark
damp places of the mind,
I could slip back
beneath the sheets of ice
to that space where water sings.

Have you heard it?

Underneath are the deeps,
where darkness makes us
sightless and ugly. Gasp,
come up for air, skate.
Skate over, skate across,
skate as if your life depended upon it.
For those are the depths
that the bucket cannot reach,
the stone thrown down
to no answering splash.

I wish I hadn't cried so much, said Alice......
Being drowned in my own tears!
That will be a queer thing to be sure!

Longing, lamentation,
the insinuating smell of mould.
Like the stain on a wall
the stain on the spirit
is a slow seepage.
She just broke down and cried.

*

It is the breaking of the waters that begins it all
and the body, like the planet,
being two-thirds liquid
what is to be done but to grieve?
Welling up, that's what we call it,
weeping, sobbing, greeting,
threnody, elegy, requiem,
willow, cypress, yew.

You ought to be ashamed of yourself, said Alice...
A great girl like you...but she went on all the same...
...shedding gallons of tears until there was
a large pool all around her.

Aquifers, reservoirs, how their consonants
eddy with the rippling sound of purpose
gathering. Under the butterflies, the eyebright,
the speedwell, under chalk, and under sandstone,
a drip, a push, a force collecting,
like shyness pushing, pushing at the spirit,
till up through the Great and Inferior Oolites,
the Corallian and Lincolnshire Limestones,
the rill, the beck and the cataract come babbling.

*

It is the breaking of the waters that begins it all.

Like ice releasing the lake
through the tender pressure of a mallard,
so the sudden opening of that cosy reservoir
sent you splashily swimming forth,
out of warm darkness into stark difference,
and now, daughter, think of that lost stream,
the one bundled up and buried
beneath this suburban road.
So much stored up to give you,
you, walking quiet beside me,
listening to that great river rush,
the future, its big noise, under ground.

The Westbourne, Tyburn, Walbrook,
the Fleet, Effra, Hydeburn,
the hidden courses, undivined,
where our feet pass.

London, where every backyard,
sparkled, if not with gold, then with ooze,
where Trafalgar Square made fountains
from the splash and glug of ancient springs,
where the density of swash and swill,
the sluice and souse of shallow wells,
could scarcely be crammed on a map
twenty-five inch to the mile.

We can follow the course
of those old lost waters
by street names in an *AtoZ*,
staunched into culverts, pipes and drains,
like the entrails of a postcode,
while the doctor who notes down
asthma attacks, in the shimmering pool
of an Apple Mac, will see that her cases
are plotted there as breathless kisses,
along the banks of concreted brooks.
The Westbourne, the Tyburn,
the Walbrook, the Fleet,

the Effra, the Hydeburn,
where our feet pass.

It is the breaking of the waters that begins it all.

*

So is the breaking of the waters
like the breaking of that tiny flask,
with its sacred essence,
the four tears of the Blessed Virgin?
That most precious phial,
carried in sunshine, in stormlight,
flood, fog and fret,
through soft days and mizzle,
mist, hail and sleet
to the monks of West Minster,
held next the heart,
by a young believer,
in frost-pinched fingers,
in fever of prayer,
a treasure revered yet finally broken.

Imagine. Journey's end.

Drenched in sun, he lies on the Heath,
floating on clover and myrtle, content,
till a second's neglect, you might call it joy,
and like dew on grass,
the four tears vanish
as if they have never been.
There are more tears then,
a boy's naked sorrow
and maybe it is the mingling of salts,
which draws forth a seeming miracle.
Where only four drops spilt
there's a magnification,
a gush, a force, a spring,
not a magnification but a magnificat,
a healing holy well,
the consolation of the Madonna,
a cure and then a curiosity,

guiding first pilgrims then tourists
to the famous spa of Hampstead.

That's how they came,
the devout, the desperate,
to the spots where a hidden source
danced so lively that the smallest stir
of any damp hillside might draw forth
the dazzle and succour of water.
Here they made villages,
found gods of the wayside
or saints and their stories
that might make us all better.
Some waters bubbled, gurgled
and gushed, some dribbled, slowed
or slithered away. Some were broken
by something like land, dammed,
ditched, diked and drained.

It is the breaking of the waters that begins it all.

Look hard you might find
the lip of a well, now hidden
beneath a cobweb of frost,
mosses and silt, crutches and votives
from the hundreds who came
with their bundle of sorrows,
tied like a knot in the pit
of the stomach and under them,
deeper, three golden heads bobbing.

*

What does it mean when a well runs dry?

So, here at my door a window cleaner
wants to refill his bucket of water
and I will carry the pail
like that most precious phial,
a twist of glass that held the tears
that washed the feet of Christ.
I will swing open my ordinary faucet,

spill the slops of everyday life
down the drain, out to the sewers,
swill the blood from the sink,
the stains from the sheet,
and call on those saints
Brigid, Anne, Winifred,
whose faith was as knowledge,
an awakening, a promise,

a splash of cold water to the face.